www.finishinglinepress.com

Stop and Smell the Fractals

(and Everything in Between)

poems by

Caroline Jennings

Finishing Line Press
Georgetown, Kentucky

Stop and Smell the Fractals

(and Everything in Between)

ACKNOWLEDGMENTS

I'd like to send my gratitude to the editors and magazines who supported
earlier versions of a few of these poems through the following publications
where they first appeared, sometimes in different forms and/or under
different original titles:

The Diamond Line: "The Music of My Newest Nephew"
Black Moon Magazine: "reduce"
Tupelo Quarterly: "The Chambered Nautilus"

Publisher: Leah Huete de Maines
Editor: Christen Kincaid
Cover Art: Jessica Jennings
Author Photo: Andrea Pruitt
Cover Design: Elizabeth Maines McCleavy

Order online: www.finishinglinepress.com
also available on amazon.com

Author inquiries and mail orders:
Finishing Line Press
PO Box 1626
Georgetown, Kentucky 40324
USA

Contents

The Chambered Nautilus: Revamped
after Oliver Wendell Holmes Sr.

one day in the aquarium I ignored
the little tank of long-legged (tentacled?)
jellyfish and even passed the tank of sharks

with sticky little-kid fingers pressed up
to the thick glass and walked all the way to
you, you little architect, and I thought

of the way you left the second to the last
temple for a new home—ripe with potential—
creating such a perfect golden spiral,

and so I was jealous. maybe it's unfair
to compare myself to a sea creature,
but nonetheless my *low-vaulted past* hangs far

over me, with last spring as an octopus
burrowing a hole into my fleshiest
parts. I found myself wringing my hands, begging

you for a lesson on building that neat wall
you know so well, the porcelain one that hides
the past, so imagine my dumbstruck surprise

when I leaned in just a tiny bit closer,
my sweat-coated forehead touching the bare glass,
and saw that your work, once pristine in my eyes,

was more like the way I sometimes
use soy milk instead of regular
in my cakes—best described as "almost,

but not quite." in fact, I'm certain
you're quite a disappointment to Ohm
and probably even Euler and Descartes

and Fermat and Pythagoras but most
importantly me, your legacy sitting in
my nightly thoughts, the ones that cling

to me as I lay alone on my bed, a stack
of old letters on the shelf mocking
me with their crookedness.

Eustress

The snake plant has started to bloom again.
Rare, so I feel lucky, like I've accomplished
something. Between the tall, sturdy leaves
sprouts small, smelly, white—fragile—flowers.

I've started, maybe once a week,
looking to some image or dream
or prompt to pull any fruit—
sticky, sweet, sour—from the roots.

Thing is, with that large plant of mine,
the only way to get those flowers
is through perfect neglect—the pessimistic
way of saying the exact amount of care.

But that's what it is (I hope).
You work little by little until some
stinky thing you've waited for claws
its way into the world.

ode to my stolen parking spot

I see you, stranger in 296, forcing me
to park all the way in 298, giving me
(unfortunately) more time to think
over the tasks of the day on the walk
to my apartment, reminding me that I need
to schedule a meeting for wednesday
and use up the rest of the bag of spinach
before tomorrow and also review
that video lecture over Dedekind cuts
for the advanced calc course that I hate
(but tell myself I can't hate, as an effort
to keep my head above water)
so at the very least, stranger,
I think you should stop and explain
if cuts are infinite or not and how I can
use them to make something real
because to me they seem to go on forever
regardless of how many steps I take away
from 298, but maybe I'm just being irrational
so instead I'll go as far as to say thank you
for the extra steps that I can use to try
and figure out when to practice piano
before my next lesson and when to call
my grandma before she goes to bed
and how to exhale in a way that really feels
right while finally opening the door to the hall
and making sure it doesn't get caught
on the frame, or maybe hoping that it does,
just so it finally stops squeaking
back and forth
over and over

you told me to think about life

as a game of blackjack—to imagine
that it was New Year's Eve and we were back
in that casino playing over and over again
and, at times, losing: having those days
where the bags under my eyes drag the rest
of me down with them, but winning
sometimes, too: walking with a friend
in the park, grabbing a dog's face in my hands
and rocking it back and forth, our tails
both wagging—two realities fluctuating
until I eventually end the game with a grand.
I was tired and told you we needed to sleep,
but instead you asked me if I would keep playing
the game, despite the holes in my blankets
and my hair falling out. I told you that yes,
in theory it would all be worth it,
and that I would spend hours
asking, "What does the book say?"
and reaching twenty only to have the dealer
get twenty-one, even if I walked out
with just a ten-dollar bill, and you knew that.
That was what you expected to hear,
but I told you that it wasn't the same thing.
You brushed my hair behind my ear
and looked at me a long time, challenging
me, not knowing why it was different.
I told you I didn't care about the money
because right now I'm in hour three hundred
forty-two of the game and the dealer has won
the last ten rounds, and yes, I have enough
chips left to keep pushing, but I can't stop
reminding you and myself that I can't
remember showing up at this casino,
and that I wish I never learned how to play,
and that I can't stop looking for an exit.

I Can't Make Sense of Now
after Ezra Pound

I'm writing a pandemic poem
because I just can't seem to ignore
the fact that we're here—all statistics
against us, life hitting us like a ton
of variables, some specifically selected
kinds of bricks—to act
together in the worst of ways
and so today I tried to go on a walk
and do my laundry and make some new
kind of soup to warm me inside
and out but the day just wasn't
full enough even though
yesterday seemed too full
and it suddenly feels hard
to believe that there is some delicate
standard model governing me and you
and the man walking on the sidewalk
below me, alone and double-masked,
off his hole-punched couch for the first time
in a week—and you know that model
is probably all shaken-up by his rise—
but right now there are wasps
outside my window throwing their bodies
at the glass in a violent, thought-
less way, ignoring the warmth
of the breeze they fly through
and the tender hold of the clouds
around them, trying to join me as I sit
alone in my living room thinking
about how each and every
day with high probability my *life slips*
by like a field mouse, not shaking
the grass that's still here despite us,
untouched by the bricks
while we stand above believing
we are the ones who let it grow.

Fibonacci Poem #1 for the Chambered Nautilus

Build
me
a wall,
one like yours,
thick and sturdy bone—
close yesterday from tomorrow,
force my eyes towards the waiting, sunny sprouts of now.

disjoint

in set theory terms I would
say my brain and my body have no elements
in common

i'm here sitting on a bench in the park
and i can't feel the wind against
my face   the sun burning my eyes or the dirt

that snuck its way into the little space
between   my toes and my leather
sandals but the long-haired happy
dog across the way is bounding
towards me and i think
maybe i could react,

catch the ball and throw
it, but instead my hands stay numb

and flat against the wood
while i squint at the sky. do you ever
stop and think about the way your brain should

work like a bunch of little plugged-in
nerves   talking to each other in a way
that makes you grab your love's face and pull
it close   or pinch a basil leaf

off of its stem in the right way as to not kill
it because right now i think my wires
are twisted and turned every which way inside
me

and my little machine needs a reboot
after what:

a walk to the park, a long
night of sitting on my comfortable couch

but nonetheless i'm here   i think   and i see
the wires from the tree in front of me
without their cable-dividers: knotted
and shoved into the ground, sucking
from deep in the earth, and i'm sitting jealous
with my grounded feet and unplugged brain.

Asymptote

I think about how good posture is important and how my back
is curved like a C at the same time. So, I tilt it back, thinking
about how not thinking about my spine makes things both worse
and better. During lunch I look out the window and watch
a waiter smoking across the street, taking deep puffs, taking time,
and I think that he probably isn't working too hard either, probably
just enough to earn twenty percent, but then again, I see how he's
whittling that cigarette away slowly and carefully, one might say
perfectly. Savoring. That's what he's doing—not just passing time,
but instead lightly holding that cigarette and coaxing it gently
into his lungs, not letting a drop of it free but the ashes, the parts
he doesn't need. Deliberately, until he reaches the end.
He reaches the end. Yeah, that's the stuff.

Don't dream of bathing
in the sun's warmth—find comfort
in thick, frozen rain.

ode to the overlooked

constant. something stays
in an equation, regardless
of what you do or what
else happens over time.

i'm not sure what to do
with that definition
as i look at myself
in the mirror tonight i see
my stomach, much softer
than last year, my right eye
drooping lower than my left,
my hair, dead but somehow
longer, thin but fighting
to take up more space,
and i damn the variables.

later, my body fighting sleep,
i wrap my arms around my middle,
burrow my feet into the sheet
(there's some evidence that warming
your feet sends a signal
to your brain to sleep,
so i burrow) and i ignore
the ticklish part of my side,
the sound i make when i yawn,
the sheep, little and white,
that i've always counted.

complementary

imagine my delight at spotting those two
whom I shall call nora and harry, their display
distracting me from the little fantasy book
I found myself exploring, then abandoning,
in the café of the bookstore when I spotted
the sharing of a small coffee between the pair,
her even and him odd, negative and positive,
imaginary and real, fitting together
the way one solves an equation by finding
the perfect value for a variable, this time,
in particular, made obvious by the way
their hands are meeting next to the mug
in a casual, delicate manner. I think they both represent
the value x—not one is the solution but both,
which could be better represented
by an integral and a derivative of one value,
or maybe explained by a function,
her tortoise-shelled glasses the pre-image
to that transfixed look on his face, the image,
let x=nora and f(x)=harry—or the reverse, or both—
depending on what you're solving.
bottom line: I'm thankful for the way he brushes her
hair out of the frame of her glasses, and the way their
laughter blends into one uniform wave function,
and the way it reminds me of you.

an ode to your morning self

not that it is any better
than your normal, natural
self but nonetheless
this can be
a praise to the skin
on the back of your neck
cupped in my hand and
your warm arms and
face against the cold
of the morning and
the crust of your eyes
and then again a praise
of how, despite the morning
clouds nearing release,
your lips call mine closer,
and how, despite the way
you question the rise,
you smile—at the sun
and at me—your lids
half-shut and your limbs
up to the ceiling

patterns

at 5:59 am the sun returns to its post in the sky
and a few minutes later the cardinals start
their morning songs and I continue to sleep through
it, probably moving flat on my back at that point
but then just 3 and a half hours later I'm up
and stretching with my rattlesnake plant

whose wavy limbs nearly reach a nearby dumbcane plant.
ten minutes post-rise I open my blinds to the sky
and notice that the little morning glories are up
and at 'em and the water on the stove has started
to boil. I've put 3 eggs in when the hour hand points
to 10 and the squirrel has climbed 30 trees: thorough.

at noon, as I walk to lunch, I have to move through
a Japanese maple stretching—regardless of its planted
roots near the sidewalk—across my path and pointing
to the sun at its highest point, begging for the sky's
light even still when I walk from lunch and start
my way towards the university, panting up

the hill and walking next to the same upperclassman
I see every Thursday, a blue and white scarf tied through
her thick blonde hair and her daily Converse finally starting
to lose their soles. later, around 4:30, I've planted
myself under one of the old oak trees and noted the sky
between the branches, and am feeling, at this point,

ready for a nap, which is quickly rejected by the point
of a thick, ancient root in my back, stuck up
between my shoulder blades, pulling my eyes from the sky
and towards the line of black ants moving through
the field and back towards their oak tunnels, this plant
only acting as civil engineering as they begin

their night routine, moving me with a slight start
from the tree and—just in time—pointing
me in the direction of home to water plants,
at least the ones that are thirsty, if their leaves have up
and dried or died or shriveled before I move through
the motions of dinner with the darkening sky.

finally, the rattlesnake plant has started to close up
as I lay, watching the hour hand point through
the 10, ready to dig us free when the sun returns to the sky.

Life as a Function Where x=Time
To my very first nephew

Let the function begin
as showing your little hands
grasping dozens
of dinosaur figurines.
I remember you—giggling
and proud—as we scratched
up the hardwood floor together,
smashing their little plastic
legs against it, snarling
like animals ourselves.

Let x increase
to show you wearing that too-large
t-shirt backwards to bed, just because
you wanted the design on the front.
When we camped in the backyard
on your ninth birthday, you held
a stuffed blue alligator through
the night and your laugh woke me
with the sunrise.

Let x increase again.
It feels almost exponential,
your way of changing.
Last month you asked me
if you could drive my car,
saying you had practiced—
that you had held a steering
wheel in your hands like I once
held you in my lap, wrapping
a towel around your post-bath body.

We sold those dino figurines years ago.
I know you forgot about them,
but last month I saw a little boy
in my passenger seat, smiling at me,
his four-year-old mouth forming
the word *parasaurolopholus*
as I handed him my keys.

What I Mean When I Say I Don't Know

Lately, when I think of my own thoughts,
an image comes to mind.
Picture this: a swampy type place,
green and blue swirls, bubbles,
greyish and juicy looking,
backswimmers climbing on top.

Around them: lady bugs,
their colors bright and lively,
and right next to them
the damsel flies, just brown,
nothing special in comparison,
but delicate, knowing their place.

When you asked me to explain
why I was upset today, my mind
went to the alligator gar
deep in that water, to your
brow-furrowed expression
last week in the backseat.

What came out was a mix
of the orange and white spotted
koi, the broken branches
on the banks, the spiny legs
of water bugs; an inept fist
thrust in, grabbing without thought.

My friend, the problem
is that when I look at you,
your kind face and concerned eyes,
my mind only shows me
a mosquito and a swallowtail,
and I don't know which one is me.

Fibonacci Poem #2 for Womanhood

Brash,
mild,
cheery.
I've placed each
me in front of you—
which one of her can you swallow?
which wraps her vines around your skull, saying *I'm here?*

Muscle Memory

Sometimes music stays in your hands
as you play. Muscles flow, no force, only insight,
as your mind wanders without a plan,

flying off-note to some dissonant land
filled with cacophony. Safe and held-tight,
sometimes music stays in your hands

while the rest of you tries to understand
a note deep in the snarl of your brain. Tonight,
my mind wanders without a plan

and lingers on a man. I leave the music stand
to think of his voice, thick with bite,
the music still staying in my hands

as I remember his commands
and my legs, stiff as deadwood on that night
when my mind wandered without a plan.

Although I falter here, the notes withstand;
my mind writhes back to me, my limbs light.
Sometimes music clings to my hands,
even as my mind wanders without a plan.

Fibonacci Poem #3 for Shining Too Bright

Put-
ting
things simp-
ly I'm won-
dering if the gold-
en scarab beetles have aware-
ness of their metallic skin, and if—to avoid ad-
ornment on some slender neck—they'd dull their shine with mud: forgotten, lonely, but at peace.

Survival Mode

I'm throwing my acorns off my limbs,
focusing my mind on where the soil
lets my roots fatten and the worms swim
through, much too deep to spoil
my route but nonetheless there, admired
by me. When I'm not a winter-bound tree
throwing—recklessly—I'm still, tired,
clinging to my cup of white tea,
full of cream and honey and linger-
ing lemon peel and sugar and sea
salt and worms and I'm digging my fingers
into the cup, scouting for a sweet
sticky paste to sow the earth to my feet.

Sting

One thing I should make clear
is that I can't handle the idea of death.
The event itself—that's manageable.
But ten years later she still haunts me,
her ghost following me around the foyer,
squeaking through in white
tennis shoes and plaid button-ups,
glasses hit with a glare.

When I was younger and climbed up in her lap,
I always noticed the pin-sized hole
on her wrinkled forehead.
She'd make a joke out of it, saying
that a horse fly, or some other winged creature
I've forgotten, left a permanent mark
on her—whether kiss
or curse, she wasn't sure.

Later, as a punchline, her diagnosis
came in the form of a wasp sting
to the eye, a gentle push to the doctor
revealing the real hive inside her skull.
Tonight, in the backyard, the buzz
of a bumblebee comes faint,
almost human, almost her,
left behind in a memory.

What I Mean When I Say Don't Go: A Contrapuntal

I walked a little slower through the hallway
                         her crossword puzzles in my back pocket

her voice stuck in my throat
                         your hand on my back—even softer than normal

I remember my small hands shaking
                         as my mom pulled me from her diseased body

and they're shaking the same way now
                         I remember that day too well

her fragile voice, her thick glasses
                         so tonight I shake again

you grab my hand and say you love me
                         as her memory sits on my chest

I count the moles on your back
                         as you tell me about your new Body and Soul

and in that moment I'm exhaling
                         as her shadow rests in the corner

these cathedral windows look like math

there is nothing like the cut
of stained glass—sharp, beautiful—
on the wall in front of me,
its "octagonal geometry"
looming over—or so the book
in the gift shop says, telling me
there is mathematical certainty
in the image of jesus
holding a baby helping him
the way we are all helped
and have been helped
and will always be
helped but only if we don't
say shit—yes, I wrote it—
and if we do we must pull out
ten hail marys and an our father
who art in heaven and who is also
apparently holding my grandma's
hands as she lies in a hospital bed
and who happens to watch as I rock
back and forth on my tile floor
and let the stones bruise my bones
so maybe I should just pray
for understanding and maybe
say thank you—yes,
thank you—for the lack
of an ability to solve
for the reds and blues
and greens in front of me
and say it makes sense,
and that the squared
prism, the perfect
vertices, the loving savior
we all know and trust
certainly belong
next to one another
in the same place.
I'm sure of it—
pass me the hymnal.

red

so much in my child-
hood room was red
the table that held
my box tv
my big fluffy
bedspread
the buttons
on my headboard
but not the walls
never the walls
because red
is too angry
and concrete
gray is perfect
for a 12-year-old
who rests
her eyes
on the floor
as she walks
through rooms
and comments
about her soul
being a dark
dark shadow
in the way
the rest of them
can never know
and I know
her body and
her face and how
in the way
her voice carried
such a tone
made you ignore
her but that gray
room knew her best
saw the sweet rose and
cherry blossom
inside her
knew her to be
in the way

she clutched
the cream carpet
her fingers tight

reduce

as of late
my bones remind
me that they can't
hold me up
even now in my backyard

my hair blending
with the dirt
irises into blue
berry fractals
lips kissing
the crepe myrtle
blood flowing
into the pond
swirling
like violet
skin lining
the trees
an ashy bark
organs
acting
as fertilizer
to a fiddle
leaf
fig

how blissful of me
to ignore the
crepe myrtle cries
and instead picture
the sun's usual
shift that will finally
hopefully feed all of me

how bold
of me to find
existence
clean

Fibonacci Poem #4 for How Not to Drown

Dive:
breath
stacking
one by one
as you spiral down
slow, your lungs tired and too full
but please listen close: don't resist the urge—no, drink deep
the thick navy waves. Taste their salt. Lay it to memory before coming up for air.

the music of my newest nephew
for Liam

there isn't much more pure than that breath
of yours, even if it does induce a sound
akin to the geese that used to chase us
in Carol Ann Cross Park, ruthless and nipping
at the backside of my nanny as she corralled
us into the car, quacking as they stomped,
quacking just like you are now as you breathe
against my chest.

I count the rhythm of the little
noises that belong to you: one and two and three
and four, then one and-a two and-a three-e-and-a,
one two and-a three four—
I never claimed it was steady—but reliable
nonetheless, that noise, in and out,
patterned and mathematical,
reminding me of your (tiny) existence.

my friend, the unsolvable

I get into your car and we head to the gallery, all while I,
not planning on the quiet calm that your vehicle
provides alongside Katy Perry's voice, keep my eyes
on the dotted lines in the road, also not planning
on the comfortableness of our *us* compared
to only yesterday when I forced at least twelve degrees
between us and found myself wanting to dive deep
into a textbook for answers. No—instead of that, we walk
through the exhibits today and note a little heart-shaped prayer
packet, your favorite of the craft wall, and imagine my surprise as you later
admire some alien-shaped piece of modern art, not because you understand
it, but specifically because you don't—and to be fair, me neither—
yet I look at that fragile tapestry made of clay and buttons
and old yarn and see, simultaneously, the way you fidget
during movies that gets on my nerves and also our walk
through the garden when we shared the chai and paused to smile
at the golden retriever bounding by and how after that when a stranger
asked you about the difference between an IPA and an APA
and you simply said you didn't know, but told me he was a nice guy,
despite the way complete strangers sometimes make you roll
your eyes, and now I'm getting that feeling that I sometimes
have when I'm solving some differential equation,
maybe a partial, and I don't know
what it's applying to, but I know I have the right answer.
so really all I can do is leave you with a simple *what?* and a
welcome back, I missed you.

Tea

When I was just a little
girl I learned that days
beginning or ending with hot tea
were always good ones,
my sweet-smelling house
filled with distant women

who served the lady-
like drink with just a little
sugar and milk—a home-
made delicacy—my daily
belly filled with options of leaves, one
box stacked on another, no tea

better than the last. Each simply tea.
Before that, my mom bloomed in her
childhood home full of mostly men, an only
daughter, first unoxidized, then with a bit
of beige, and then a glowing brown—her daily
cup steeping her well. Eventually her dorm

and then apartment and finally home
smelled of English Breakfast—
a mandatory start or end to her day
as a doctor and single mother,
while my oldest sister was small
and her narrow limbs comprised the only

roots in the garden. Later, the other seedlings and I
sat in the kitchen of my mom's newest home,
still fresh and bright green, always asking her for a little
more sugar—maybe two cubes—with our tea,
the thing we shared, us tiny women
with our flower-painted cups. Those days

are stuck in my mind today
like honey in a mug, each one
reminding me that a young woman—
still laced with green—alone in an apartment,
her chest warmed by masala chai,
her hands strong but still small

and feminine, can dwell on a place
where one shares both loneliness and tea
wrapped up in women while the day is still young.

my memories as clouds

nothing halts their drift
each one different

like a sheep or flower or
the look of my year-long face

tight and
creviced

I think one is missing
and I can't remember

its exact shape
but I search anyway

for this big bundle
of shadow that did

me no favors
and I wonder why

I'm looking
thinking that maybe I want

to squeeze it 'til
it finally runs clear

but instead I can only see the one
that looks like a precious laugh

slipping out my bedroom window or
another shaped like the way I'm restored

by the scent of fresh shallots and
suddenly I don't really miss

the condensation of why
and what I hated anymore.

the great steak off

butter and garlic and jus on the stove,
every square foot of the student apartment
painted thick with cowboy-ribeye smell,
a scent that won't leave my hair after one
wash, but maybe two, complimented
well by the little hill of mashed potatoes
that I'm responsible for, the one that inspired
us to do our little mashed potato dance
in unison, you and I, and there we were
after more than three years and fistfuls
of steaks and potatoes with our arms in the air
and our hips moving back and forth in
a silly little pendulum pattern matching
the ebb and flow of our meals and movies
and tense silences and the sine-like consistency
of the look in your eyes when you see me
in the evenings (we're at the peaks now)

do you remember when you saw those leaves
swirling in the street freshman year,
"like an integral, see?"
I think that's us: up-and-down,
swirling around, continuous

Fibonacci Poem #5 for Kissing

after Ross Gay

Gold
finch
pecking
delicate
blooms, a corolla
of petals, the sweet symmetry,
the odd evenness, the thickness of dripping nectar.

With Thanks

I have received an abundance of support and inspiration throughout the writing of this collection, and I am very thankful for everyone who has helped along the way.

I'd like to first send my appreciation to Geffrey Davis, whose work has captivated and inspired me long before we met. Your feedback, advice, and constant encouragement are an integral part of my growth as a poet, and I owe many of my poems to you.

I would also like to thank Dr. Mark Arnold, who has guided me in my exploration of the Gram-Schmidt process for the past few years. You have provided me with a window into the exciting world of mathematics research, which undoubtedly inspired a great deal of this collection.

I would also like to acknowledge Dr. Sidney Burris, whose course on British and Irish Postcolonial Literature introduced me to writers like Seamus Heaney, a constant inspiration. The wealth of knowledge you provided in the course has developed me as a student, writer, and human.

I'd like to thank Joshua Luckenbach for providing me with a wonderful introduction to poetry, and Landon McGhee for making me rethink everything I thought I knew.

Finally, I'd like to thank Alex Siebenmorgen, Rheana Davenport, Perry Rickard, and countless others who were always willing to give my poems a quick read or help me deconstruct my thoughts.

www.ingramcontent.com/pod-product-compliance
Lightning Source LLC
Chambersburg PA
CBHW020221090426
42734CB00008B/1167